Rapha's Touch: Healing from Sexual Abuse

Rapha's Touch: Healing from Sexual Abuse

JoAnn Streeter Shade

Gracednotes Ministries

Gracednotes Ministries

425 East Walnut Street

Ashland, Ohio 44805

Printed in the United States

ISBN: 13: 978-1481181877
ISBN-10: 1481181874

DEDICATION

to the midwives of the soul, who bring life through pain

CONTENTS

Weave in faith and God will find the thread.

1

TO MEND

As my sufferings mounted I soon realized that there were two ways in which I could respond to my situation - either to react with bitterness or seek to transform the suffering into a creative force. I decided to follow the latter course.
Martin Luther King Jr.

TO REMEMBER

When I was a child, my mother had a round, wooden mending basket with hand-painted hearts and flowers that sat by her chair in the living room. Many nights, as the family gathered to watch television, she would reach into her basket and begin to repair our clothing. Her tasks were usually simple: a missing button to reattach, a torn seam to stitch together, a sock to darn, or the worn knees of my father's work pants to patch. A few carefully placed stitches and the garment was functional once again.

To my sorrow, she was not always successful in her rescue of damaged clothing. Our family photo album holds a snapshot of a beaming nine-year-old girl with bouncing pigtails, wearing a black corduroy jumper accented by a candy-cane striped blouse. I wore that favorite outfit quite often, and one day, in my haste to head off to the adventures of the neighborhood, I failed to change my clothing after school. The backyard fence was the quickest access route to the neighbor's yard, and it was there that my beloved jumper caught on the fence post and suffered a massive tear. Whatever punishment I received for my carelessness is long-forgotten, but the destruction of that jumper is imprinted on my mind, for not even the most skilled seamstress could have salvaged that outfit.

That torn jumper stands as a symbol for what later became torn in me through sexual abuse. The man who abused me set me up, honed in to the adolescent stirrings in my heart, and then deliberately and destructively crossed the line with me sexually. It was a betrayal of my body, my trust, and my heart. The fabric ripped again, but this time what was torn was the fabric of my soul.

Sexual abuse has long-lasting, life-altering consequences, but these consequences do not have to be life-destroying. Surrounded by the gracious presence of Jehovah-Rapha, the God who heals, my personal story of abuse found healing through the hard work of therapy and the passage of time, but, like other wounds, the scars of sexual abuse never fade away completely.

These pages are offered to those who have been wounded through the abuse of others, as well as to those who walk beside them and love them. They come with the prayer that the healing touch of Jehovah-Rapha will be received in its fullness. These words provide a framework for thinking about the redeeming nature of God through the metaphor of needlework, the sewing together of that which has been torn apart.

Each chapter begins with a glimpse from my own memory that may help you name the feelings present in the aftermath of sexual abuse. As you hear bits of my life story, take time to remember a part of your story that fits into the theme of the chapter. The details of your story may differ from mine, but the journey of healing begins at the same place – in the presence of Jehovah-Rapha, the One who heals. Remember, too, that as much as the abuse may have colored your life story, you are so much more than the abuse, so much more than a victim.

The snapshots of memory will be interwoven with the story line of Tamar, daughter of King David, whose sexual abuse at the hands of her brother has been recorded in the Old Testament. Each chapter will also include sections of information about sexual abuse, questions to spur your thinking and remembering, prayers for your use to direct your conversation with God, and a series of action verbs that invite you to put your thoughts and feelings into tangible expressions of art and movement. Finally, you will also find resources for further exploration, as well as words of comfort and challenge from the Scriptures and from the voices of those who understand the healing power of God.

JEHOVAH-RAPHA

The invitation to healing is extended by Almighty God, also known in the Hebrew as Jehovah-Rapha, the One who heals, or literally, "who mends," the One who knows how to sew together that which has been torn. Found in Exodus 15, this name for God is self-proclaimed: "I am the Lord who heals you," as the NLT tells us. Unlike El-Roi, the God who sees, a name given to God by Hagar, it is the Lord who speaks this name to the people of Israel: *this is who I am.*

The context in which this name was first spoken is fascinating in its implications for those in need of healing and hope. Following a period of slavery and abuse under the reign of the Pharoah, the Israelites have escaped from Egypt in a dramatic rescue, and Miriam the prophet(the sister of Moses and Aaron) has just led the people in song: "Sing to the Lord, for he is highly exalted" (Exodus 15:21). Moses then led them away from the Red Sea and into the desert of Shur.

The word Shur means 'wall,' and it appears that in the desert of Shur the people of God have hit a wall. They may have expected their deliverance to be immediate, yet now that they've crossed the Red Sea, they're faced with the wide expanse of desert and no relief in sight. We can almost hear their frustration: *We thought our pain was over – we're free from the abuse of the Pharoah, but now we're just as bound by this empty desert.*

With no map or memory of this new land, they travel for three days without finding water. When they finally find it at Marah, it is too bitter to drink, perhaps reflecting their own bitterness at feeling abandoned to the desert.

After Moses cried out to the Lord on behalf of the people, he was instructed to throw a piece of wood into the water, and the water became good to drink. It was at Marah, the place of bitterness, that the Lord used this revealing phrase, "I am the Lord who heals you," Jehovah-Rapha.

And after Marah? The people of God traveled to the oasis of Elim, where they found twelve springs and seventy palm trees, and they were able to camp beside the water.

This passage of the exodus of a people can serve as an image for the journey of a woman coming out of the arms of sexual abuse. The abuse is over (the people are out of Egypt), but the desert awaits, with the fear, anger, sorrow and thirst found in the aftermath of the abuse. There are times in the healing journey where it seems we're up against a wall (Shur) and can't find any relief. We weep bitter tears when we realize that while the physical abuse has ended, the pain has not vanished.

When we do reach out, sometimes the water is bitter. "Get on with it," our pastor tells us. "Just give it to God." "That was ten years ago," our friend says. "Can't you get over it?" "Why are you so cold to me?" our husband asks. "Be quiet. Don't take this thing to heart," repeats the Absalom in our family (see Tamar's story). We attempt to drink of the water of relationships, but sometimes the abuse is repeated, and we find ourselves growing bitter as we look for love in all the wrong places.

Yet Jehovah-Rapha is present. When we cry out to the Lord, we find the water that refreshes, that heals. When what is bitter is named and faced, the sweetness of grace begins to overcome what has been harsh.

The image at the end of the passage is Elim, a place of hope and abundance, of shade and sustenance. Elim is a place of twelve springs, enough water to share with others. There are also seventy palm trees in Elim, with their nourishing fruit and their protection from the sun's blazing rays. And through it all, there is Jehovah-Rapha, present and powerful.

TAMAR'S STORY LINE

Throughout these pages, we will spend time with Tamar, the daughter of King David and his wife Maacah, as her story connects to our stories. Tamar belonged to the royal family, yet her position in the palace did not prevent her from becoming the victim of incestuous rape. Tamar was sexually abused, and her abuse is recorded on the pages of the Bible for all the world to read, to see, to hear and to remember. Here is her story as found in II Samuel 13, from Today's New International Version.

Amnon and Tamar

In the course of time, Amnon son of David fell in love with Tamar, the beautiful sister of Absalom son of David.

[2] Amnon became so obsessed with his sister Tamar that he made himself ill. She was a virgin, and it seemed impossible for him to do anything to her.

[3] Now Amnon had an adviser named Jonadab son of Shimeah, David's brother. Jonadab was a very shrewd man. [4] He asked Amnon, "Why do you, the king's son, look so haggard morning after morning? Won't you tell me?"

Amnon said to him, "I'm in love with Tamar, my brother Absalom's sister."

[5] "Go to bed and pretend to be ill," Jonadab said. "When your father comes to see you, say to him, 'I would like my

sister Tamar to come and give me something to eat. Let her prepare the food in my sight so I may watch her and then eat it from her hand.'"

⁶ So Amnon lay down and pretended to be ill. When the king came to see him, Amnon said to him, "I would like my sister Tamar to come and make some special bread in my sight, so I may eat from her hand."

⁷ David sent word to Tamar at the palace: "Go to the house of your brother Amnon and prepare some food for him." ⁸ So Tamar went to the house of her brother Amnon, who was lying down. She took some dough, kneaded it, made the bread in his sight and baked it. ⁹ Then she took the pan and served him the bread, but he refused to eat.

"Send everyone out of here," Amnon said. So everyone left him. ¹⁰ Then Amnon said to Tamar, "Bring the food here into my bedroom so I may eat from your hand." And Tamar took the bread she had prepared and brought it to her brother Amnon in his bedroom. ¹¹ But when she took it to him to eat, he grabbed her and said, "Come to bed with me, my sister."

¹² "No, my brother!" she said to him. "Don't force me! Such a thing should not be done in Israel! Don't do this wicked thing. ¹³ What about me? Where could I get rid of my disgrace? And what about you? You would be like one of the wicked fools in Israel. Please speak to the king; he will not

keep me from being married to you." ¹⁴ But he refused to listen to her, and since he was stronger than she, he raped her.

¹⁵ Then Amnon hated her with intense hatred. In fact, he hated her more than he had loved her. Amnon said to her, "Get up and get out!"

¹⁶ "No!" she said to him. "Sending me away would be a greater wrong than what you have already done to me."

But he refused to listen to her. ¹⁷ He called his personal servant and said, "Get this woman out of my sight and bolt the door after her." ¹⁸ So his servant put her out and bolted the door after her. She was wearing a richly ornamented robe, for this was the kind of garment the virgin daughters of the king wore. ¹⁹ Tamar put ashes on her head and tore the ornamented robe she was wearing. She put her hands on her head and went away, weeping aloud as she went.

²⁰ Her brother Absalom said to her, "Has that Amnon, your brother, been with you? Be quiet for now, my sister; he is your brother. Don't take this thing to heart." And Tamar lived in her brother Absalom's house, a desolate woman.

²¹ When King David heard all this, he was furious. ²² And Absalom never spoke to Amnon again; he hated Amnon because he had disgraced his sister Tamar.

TO UNDERSTAND

Healing. Can what is tragically torn within us ever be mended? That question screams for an answer in the lives of women who have been sexually abused or assaulted, whether as a child, adolescent or adult. These are rips to our souls, damage inflicted upon us by another, that is beyond the mending abilities of our mother's touch or our feeble attempts at self-repair. "Time heals all wounds" is a curse to us, rather than a promise. Time may have allowed a thin scab to form over the open wound, but it tends to be one that is easily ripped open again when we least expect it. The scent of aftershave or the feel of a certain piece of furniture can send us twenty, thirty, even forty years into the past, and the terror of our abuse is present tense, front and center.

These pages have been created for those who have suffered this deeply disturbing offense. They are offered in the firm belief that what has been so wickedly torn in us can be restored to wholeness by the power of the Lord God, the support of caring people, and the courage of the woman who is open to seek after that healing.

Please note that while sexual abuse can be perpetrated on boys and men, this particular resource is focused on sexual abuse as experienced by girls and women.

YOUR STORY

The aftermath of sexual abuse is different for each person who has experienced that pain. Its effect is not always logical, nor is it always proportional to the level of invasion. One woman may recover quickly from rape, while a teen-age girl may wrestle for years with an experience of being groped by a cousin in the movie theater. Each woman responds according to her circumstances, her personality, her own internal strength, and the response of those she entrusts with her story.

The desire for healing from the ravages of sexual abuse is not selfish or foolish. Not only does such healing bring a sense of internal peace, but it also can change the legacy we bequeath to future generations.

Reasons to heal. Consider the following list of reasons to heal. Add as many others as you want. Choose the one which is most important to you just now and claim it as your own.

1. I can look at myself in the mirror and not turn away.

2. My children will not be burdened with my shame.

3. I can have a healthier relationship with the man in my life.

4. I can be used to bless another in the name of Christ.

5. I won't cry myself to sleep at night.

6. I can enjoy being a woman.

7. God's glory can be shown in my healing.

8. The anger and pain resulting from my abuse will no longer be the driving force of who I am.

THIMBLES

One of the essentials in my mother's sewing basket was a thimble. I'm not sure that I even own one, but she found the use of a thimble indispensable for protecting her finger as she sewed on a button or fixed a fallen hem., keeping her safe from the random needle prick. I'm suggesting a few "thimbles" that can be used as protections against the despair and discouragement that can threaten to halt our journey. Rather than display these thimbles in a decorative case, put them on as needed.

THIMBLE #1. Know that **this path is difficult**. There will be times when you may feel angry, frightened, or sorrowful. Acknowledge those feelings, share them with a trusted friend, bring them to God in prayer, but do not let them keep you stuck. Have courage.

THIMBLE #2. **Don't walk alone**. It is essential to have support in walking this journey. Find someone to provide that to you. Possible choices are a counselor, a trusted friend, your spouse, or a support group or therapy group. Lean on them when you need to. Choosing professional help is a wise decision when faced with the memories of sexual abuse, for skilled, godly counselors, social workers and psychologists can use their experiences and training to strengthen the work you're doing, and you can even share what you're discovering on these pages with them. If you are not able to get that support, be sure to have someone that can be on the watch for danger signs such as self-destructive behaviors and suicidal thoughts, and who will intervene to get you help if those occur.

THIMBLE #3. **Observe the four-fold way.**

> **Show up.** Be present to yourself during your work in these pages. Be willing to face what has happened.

> **Pay attention.** Pay attention to your feelings, your body, your memories, your fears, your senses and your companions. Be receptive to the moving of the Spirit of God through these days.

> **Tell the truth.** Allow yourself to hear the truth.

21

Speak the truth of your heart to God. God can handle it. Listen for the truths of God as grace is whispered to you.

Release the demand for specific outcomes. Don't try to orchestrate the process. Don't think that you know what you will look like in six months or two years. Let it happen.

See Angeles Arrien's book, *The Four-Fold Way*, for a fuller description of these concepts.

THIMBLE #4. **Seek a prayer covering**. Ask at least one person to pray specifically for you each day. You do not have to give them details unless you want to; simply ask them to bring you before the Lord. Commit to praying daily as well.

THIMBLE #5. **Take your time**. Healing occurs over a period of time. If you begin to feel overwhelmed or anxious, put on the 'trauma brakes.' Put it aside for a bit and go for a walk or wash the dishes. Check in with someone. Breathe deeply.

THIMBLE #6. Use a journal or notebook to **record your thoughts and feelings.** Take time to write down nudges and prayers that come to you. Answer the questions as outlined.

Do some of the action verb exercises on the pages of your journal. It will be good to have this record of your progress when you're faced with difficult days in the future.

THIMBLE #7. Commit to a **self-care** contract. Use this as a sample, and add the pieces which you need.

As I spend time in this book, I commit to taking care of myself.

1. If I need to talk, I will call:

2. If I am afraid I will hurt myself, I will call one of the following: crisis center, counselor/group leader, friend, emergency room, 9-1-1.

3. I will set aside these pages when I feel anxious or overwhelmed.

4. I will stay away from:

5. I will be good to myself. I will (choose 1, 2 or more) take a bubble bath, exercise, eat healthy food, give myself a gift, take a long walk, spend time alone, have coffee with a friend, watch a chick flick, take a nap.

ACTION VERBS

~ show up ~ pay attention ~ tell the truth ~
~ release the outcome ~

There will be a variety of opportunities to act in response to what you're reading and feeling. You'll be invited to create, write, listen, research, search, compose, meditate, color, look in the mirror, view, pray, bake, celebrate, choose, speak, release and quilt as you move through these pages. Choose what interests or intrigues you, but also take the opportunity to try something new.

Create. Prepare a journal or notebook to use as you work through these pages. Decorate its cover, set up sections for the chapters in this book, or add some pictures of girls and women to its pages.

View the movie *O Brother, Where Art Thou.* Spend time with the baptismal scene, and sing along with the seekers as they "go down in the river to pray." *O, sister, let's go down, down in the river to pray.* What do these words say to you today? What is the prayer you are praying as you hear them, sing them?

Taste something bitter today, such as dark chocolate, strong, unsweetened coffee, uncured olives, or even an aspirin dissolving on your tongue. Allow the taste to remain in your mouth for a time.

Search for a symbolic piece of wood to throw into the waters of Marah, of bitterness. Place it in a spot where you will see it from time to time, or cast it upon the river, lake or creek near your home.

Assemble your own mending basket. Include items that will help you in your time in this book such as a favorite CD, a fragrant candle, a thimble, an eye-catching box of tissues, a friend's phone number, and a piece of chocolate (or two).

PRAYER

Listen to God with a broken heart. He is not only the doctor who mends it, but also the [caring parent] who wipes away the tears.
Criss Jami

Pray the written prayer at the conclusion of each chapter. But also pray your own prayers all along the journey. You may want to seek out Catherine Foote's helpful collection, *Survivor Prayers: Talking with God About Childhood Sexual Abuse*, as well as *Guerrillas of Grace: Prayers for the Battle* by Ted Loder, for additional prayer support.

Jehovah-Rapha.
I come to you today as one who has experienced an abuse of my female body, my female soul.
Give to me the piece of wood to cast upon the bitter waters of Marah.
Lead me to the sweet waters of Elim,
the refreshment of twelve springs,
the protection and sustenance of seventy palm trees.
Let me hear your name today: I am the One who heals.
Amen and Amen.

FROM THE MENDER'S BASKET

At the close of each chapter you'll find a section that contains words to draw on from the Mender's Basket. These scripture verses, hymns and quotations are words and images of comfort and strength that you can hold onto. Picture this as a resource to reach into as needed. Do something tangible with the words that are especially meaningful to you. Copy them on an index card or post-it note. Place them above your sink or on the bathroom mirror. Make them your screen-saver. Make a mix of healing music to listen to. Memorize scripture. Frame a favorite verse. Claim the promises of God as your own.

Weave the unveiling fabric of God's Word through your heart and mind. It will hold strong, even if the rest of life unravels.
Gigi Graham Tchividjian

What I see brings grief to my soul because of all the women of my city.
Lamentations 3:51

NEW THREADS TO FOLLOW

Each chapter will provide a list of resources that are suggested for further study. While I've drawn upon my own experience and training in the preparation of this book, as well as the writings of others in this field, I am not a specialist on the subject of sexual abuse, particularly in a therapeutic sense. Some of the suggested resources do provide a more academic or research-based approach, while others suggest additional images of both the impact of sexual abuse and models of healing.

The Four Fold Way, Angeles Arrien - four simple reminders for living well.

Survivor Prayers: Talking with God About Childhood Sexual Abuse, Catherine J. Foote - poignant words of hope and healing.

Guerrillas of Grace: Prayers for the Battle, Ted Loder - a help to those who've forgotten how to talk to God.

2

UNSTAINED FABRIC

Yet the Lord longs to be gracious to you.
Isaiah 30:18

TO REMEMBER

My earliest memories are hazy but I do remember going to church with my father as a young child, probably around the age of three. My brother was an infant at that time, and my mother stayed home with him while my dad and I went to church. I have a glimpse of myself sitting in that aging sanctuary, somehow knowing that this was God's House, and wanting to be in it. I'm told that I didn't want to go to the nursery, and I wonder if that desire to be with my father in the place of worship was evidence of the earliest stirrings in my soul, that I somehow knew that being in God's House was something my heart desired, a longing to touch the holy.

Picture that little girl, the little girl that you were at age three, with her round eyes brimming with innocence. Totally innocent - of course not, for if you've spent much time with a small child, you know that even at that young age, the child is by no means totally innocent. But for most young children,

there is an innocence, a trustfulness, a purity that has been
protected from exposure to the imperfection of the world.
And whether we were three or thirteen when sexual abuse
entered our story, we experienced a loss of that innocence
that was stripped away, gone forever.

TAMAR'S STORY LINE

Tamar was born into privileged circumstances, the daughter
of David, King of Israel, and Maacah, daughter of Talmai
king of Geshur. She was royalty, young and beautiful, a princess in the palace. A virgin, the scripture tells us, dressed in a
beautiful robe, a colorful garment that signified her purity and
birth. Because of the political implications for David's family,
Tamar may have been a key figure in future alliances, and it is
possible that an arranged marriage was waiting for her in the
near future as well.

The actors in this story begin their actions from what is po-
tentially a good place, a place of good intentions. First,
Tamar's half-brother Amnon, son of David and Ahinoam
from Jezreel, fell in love with Tamar. The love of a young
man for a young woman is in itself a good thing. Unfortu-
nately for Amnon, his love was directed toward a woman
who was possibly promised to another, and who, as his half
sister, was not likely to be available to him.

A second man in this drama is a cousin, Shimeah, who's described as shrewd. Seeing Amnon's unhappiness at his inability to have Tamar as his own, Shimeah suggested a plan to bring Amnon and Tamar together. We want to help out our friends and relatives, often searching for a solution to their dilemmas – just being helpful is our motto.

Tamar's father, King David, also plays into the story, sending word to Tamar to come to her brother's side, seemingly a reasonable request when a family member is ill. He probably didn't think twice about it.

The fourth man, her brother Absalom, born to David and to Tamar's mother, received his sister into his household at the conclusion of her story, offering her the protection she needed. A good thing to do, yes? Absalom's desire for revenge feels right as well – after all, his sister had been hurt badly. Evil shouldn't go unpunished, should it? His anger was coming from a sense of love for her, wasn't it?

And Tamar? She too responded from a good heart toward her brother. She carefully prepared bread for her ill brother in response to her father's request, spoke up about the reality of the situation, and even suggested an alternative to Amnon that could have allowed for a less destructive ending to her story, and ultimately to his story.

Tamar, Amnon, Shimeah, David and Absalom. All people who were created in the image of Jehovah, all people who began (to give them the benefit of the doubt) with good intentions.

Yet all the good intentions in the world, Tamar's royal blood, and her privileged position did little to protect her from the horror of abuse at the hands of these same male relatives, for her brother and her cousin conspired to lure Tamar into Amnon's bed, her father contributed to the abuse by sending her to her brother, and Absalom did not appear to take her pain seriously. Dignity and depravity – here we have both, tied together in one story line, a story that saw alleged love turn to hate and lust turn to disgust, bringing destruction to the family of David, the one chosen by God.

Yet even in this shameful and sorrow-filled narrative, we cling to the hope that God is in it. God is in the preservation of the story, in the voice of Tamar, and in the *en-theos* (God-within) in Tamar to speak up, to suggest alternatives to violence and banishment. And God is in the redemption of Tamar's story, in the redemption of our stories.

Is it simply a coincidence that the name Tamar means palm tree? Or is there a connection between the God who reveals himself as Jehovah-Rapha, the God who heals, and Tamar, one who is like the palm tree that stood at the refreshing springs of Elim?

TO UNDERSTAND

Dignity. Within Tamar, and within each one of us, lies dignity. We are formed in the image of God. The creation account in Genesis paints that picture from the start. "Let us make human beings in our image, in our likeness."

Compassionate. Merciful. Slow to anger. Just. Loving. Creative. Dependable. Gracious. Forgiving. All words that describe the character of God, all words that describe the dignity placed within the child of God. That's the imago Dei, the image of God that we are created in.

Consider the words of dignity and creation found in Psalm 139:13-16. Read the passage out loud at least once a day while you are in this section. Claim the conviction that you are fearfully and wonderfully made in the image of God.

For you created my inmost being;
you knit me together in my mother's womb.
I praise you because I am fearfully and wonderfully made;
your works are wonderful,
I know that full well.
My frame was not hidden from you
when I was made in the secret place.
When I was woven together in the depths of the earth,
your eyes saw my unformed body.
All the days ordained for me were written in your book
before one of them came to be.

Bent toward sin. Within the little girl that we see, that we remember, and whose spirit remains within us even as adult women, lies depravity, a religious word which means we struggle with a bent toward sin. Like Amnon, we desire to be the center of our universe, and we demand to get what we want when we want it, no matter the cost to anyone else.

Healthy longings. In light of our dignity and our depravity, we also realize that healthy longings have been placed within our soul by our Creator. We are created with the desire to know and to be known, to love and to be loved, to touch and to be touched, to offer respect and to be respected, and to honor and to be honored, among other legitimate longings.

In your journal or notebook, write a sentence about how you are experiencing one of these longings in your heart today.

Wounds. In our desire to live out our longings, we discover that they are not always handled with care by another. Because of the way all people are bent toward sin, we are hurt by their actions to us. It may be in the form of a careless word or a nasty look, but it also may come as a physical attack or a deliberate crossing of our personal and sexual boundaries. Because of their carelessness, their neglect, their personal deficits, their depravity, and, yes, the evil in anoth-

34

er's heart, we are wounded by what they do to us.

To put it all together, we are made in God's image, as humans we have a bent toward selfishness and sin, we have healthy longings to be in loving relationships, and when we are in those relationships we may be wounded by others who also are bent toward sin and act that out. It seems like a mouthful of words, but dignity, depravity, longings and wounds summarize our human condition.

YOUR STORY

Think of a young girl you know. Print out a picture of her. How does she reflect the image of God in the following ways:

Compassionate. Merciful. Slow to anger. Just. Loving. Creative. Dependable. Gracious. Forgiving?

Now, move back in time. Draw upon your memory of yourself as a young girl, and see if you can discover some images of that little girl who was created in the image of God, the child who was compassionate. Merciful. Slow to anger. Just. Loving. Creative. Dependable. Gracious. Forgiving.

Now, for the third step, use the same words to look at yourself in the mirror today. How do you reflect the image of God? How are you compassionate? Merciful? Slow to anger? Just? Loving? Creative? Dependable? Gracious? Forgiving?

Spend some time connecting with these good, godly values within your heart and life.

ACTION VERBS

~ show up ~ pay attention ~ tell the truth ~
~ release the outcome ~

Create. Using pictures from magazines, your own photos, or your drawings, make a collage of faces of small children. Choose from an assortment of ages and expressions. When you complete the collage, take a few minutes to think about the innocence in which these children were born. Name the emotion you see on each face.

Write. Ruth Senter describes the consequences of sin entering the world. "Your creation creaked and groaned beneath its own weight. I creaked and groaned and disobeyed. Perfect love was forever spoiled, tainted by my self-centeredness." Write a haiku to describe your reaction to her words. A haiku is a style of a poem of three lines which has a 5-7-5 pattern of syllables. Here's an example:

creaking and groaning
wheels splash slush upon chaste snow
innocence defiled

Search. Do some detective work. Keep a notebook for a week, recording each glimpse of God you see in another person.

Compose a letter to God that describes how you feel in regards to one of the following longings.

-to be loved

-to be filled

-to be believed

-to be honored

-to be valued

-to be touched

-to be known

Meditate on Mark 10:13-16. Allow yourself to be the child in this scene. Imagine the strength of Jesus' arms, the smell of the sea on the wind. Feel his hands tussle your hair. Look into his eyes. Listen for his voice to speak your name. Breathe deeply. Enjoy being the beloved.

PRAYER

Creator God;
You knit me together in my mother's womb.
You knew the size of needles to use, and when to knit, when to purl.
You traced the intricate patterns of my fingertips with your hand.
You count the number of hairs on my head.
You discern, even before I do, the deepest desires of my heart.
You know me.
Display your image within me.
Give me the courage to plunge into the depths of my longings.
You also know when crooked stitches need to be ripped out.
Do not blind my eyes to my sin,
but allow the light that reveals it to do so kindly, gently.
I trust you, my Lord and my God, to meet me at the place of my deepest
need as I take the step of faith into these pages,
from Egypt, through Marah, to Elim.

In the name of Jesus,
Amen.

FROM THE MENDER'S BASKET

He also brought me up out of a horrible pit,
Out of the miry clay,
And set my feet upon a rock,
And established my steps.
Psalm 40:2

The road from devastation to recovery is not a quick trip down the expressway. No, this highway's markers are pain and anger, flashbacks and setbacks. But God promises that we will rise again from each obstacle and he empowers us to do so.
A New Beginning

Wait till the Lord comes.
He will bring to light what is hidden in darkness,
and will expose the motives of people's hearts.
At that time each will receive their praise from God.
I Corinthians 4:5

[We can accept] a deep and meaningful alteration, without blinding our eyes to the fact that permanent and final change awaits the transformation of the world
through Christ's return.
Dan Allender, *The Wounded Heart*

NEW THREADS TO FOLLOW

Longing for Love: A Woman's Conversations with a Compassionate Heavenly Father, Ruth Senter - just what it says it is.

Transformation Soup, Sark - a rather campy, fun treatment of ways to approach change.

Texts of Terror, Phyllis Trible - a serious look at four scripture accounts that involve harm to women.

A New Beginning: Daily Devotions for Women Survivors of Sexual Abuse (Thomas Nelson Publishers) - short readings for each day.

Les Miserables - a powerful film of redemption.

The Return of the Prodigal, Henri Nouwen - a beautiful book that focuses on our identity as the beloved of God.

3

A DAMAGED REMNANT

For he found her in the countryside,
and the betrothed young woman cried out,
but there was no one to save her.
Deuteronomy 22:27

TO REMEMBER.

When I was still sewing (back in the day) an elderly woman in our church gave me a box of fabric. When I opened it, I found that it was filled with remnants, scraps of material left over from sewing projects she had done, probably from up to 50 years before by the looks of the box. Some of the material was yellowed or stained. Other pieces were irregular scraps left when she cut out the parts of her garments. The fabric at the bottom of the box had gotten wet at some point, and it was moldy and nasty. Even if I had only been making doll clothing, there was nothing in the box that I could use. They were all useless remnants. Scraps. Good for nothing but the rag bin. When what is pure has been stained by the sin of another . . .

TAMAR'S STORY LINE

The story of Tamar, the beautiful daughter of David, the King of Israel, may have begun with good intentions on the part of the participants, but very quickly the story develops into an account of devious behavior. The story line is simple, summed up with a handful of verbs: to desire, to conspire, to deceive, to endanger, to deny, to rape. Here's what happened:

Amnon desired Tamar, even though she was his sister. Although the Scripture isn't explicit about this, my guess is that as the son of the king, Amnon was used to getting his own way.

In order to placate the king's son, Shimeah conspired with Amnon so that he could get what he wanted. Shimeah reminds me of a handler for a celebrity of some kind, such as a political candidate or a famous rock star. As Amnon's fortunes rose or fell, so did Shimeah's, so he was determined to find a way for his superstar to get what he wanted, no matter the fallout to anyone else.

In the next step in the plot, Amnon deceived David. Here was the perfect time for Amnon to stop, to realize what he was doing and what this would do to his relationship with his father. But instead, he went ahead with his lie.

And then there's David. By sending Tamar to Amnon, David endangered his daughter, although he may not have been aware of that threat. For me, the jury's out on his involvement. On one hand, did he not pay any attention to what was going on in his household? Did he not notice his lovesick son? Did he take the "boys will be boys" attitude in regards to Amnon's infatuation? Had he learned nothing from the painful aftermath of his own dalliance with Bathsheba? Or did he trust his son to tell him the truth and do what was right?

As for Tamar, she initially did what she was asked to do, both by her father/king and by her brother. That's what women were expected to do, wasn't it? Did she have any suspicions about the request? If so, the narrator doesn't mention any hesitation on her part.

I do wonder if Tamar was confused when Amnon sent everyone else away and asked her to come into his bedroom. It's possible that a flicker of doubt, a shadow of fear may have passed through her mind, but this was her brother. If you can't trust your family, who can you trust? Surely he wouldn't do anything to hurt her. Naïve? Gullible? Perhaps in hindsight, but given what was likely to be her young age and protected status as the king's daughter, her response was certainly not irresponsible or unwise.

When what Amnon had in mind became apparent to Tamar, she was quick to speak. "No." Tamar clearly denied Amnon's advances toward her. She spoke first to her relationship with him. "No, my brother," then to his place in the kingdom, "in

Israel," and finally to his morality, "don't do this wicked thing." But none of her words were persuasive, none changed his mind.

Tamar then appealed to the potential consequences, both to her disgrace and to his future, even going as far as to offer to be his bride. But nothing in what she said spoke to Amnon's heart. "He refused to listen to her, and since he was stronger than her, Amnon raped her." End of scene one.

Look at the account from the perspective of family relationships: Brother desired sister. Cousin egged on royal cousin. Son deceived father. Father (unwittingly?) set-up daughter, putting her in danger. Sister rebuffed brother's advances. Brother raped sister. And, dare we ask, where was the mother??? No mention of her, not of her complicity, her impotence or her rage.

I looked up the word *rape* in the thesaurus, searching for a synonym that would fit the "d" pattern of desire, deception, danger and denial, but there were no other words listed for rape in the thesaurus provided on the computer when I pressed shift/F7. That served as a harsh reminder to me that when rape occurs, there are no words to pretty it up, to tidy up the damage, to ignore the pain. Rape, and all other forms of sexual abuse, are heinous acts, an assault against body and soul. Here it is, straight off the page in the Bible. Tamar was raped.

One additional thought. James B. Jordan has created a time-line for David's life, and he suggests that at the time of Tamar's rape, Amnon would have been 19 or 20 and Absalom about 18. As the unmarried sister, Tamar is likely to have been just at puberty – perhaps 14 or 15. There may have been an arranged marriage waiting for her, leaving the window for Amnon's advances to be quite small. While it doesn't excuse their actions, their young ages do help to explain Amnon's self-centered scheming, Absalom's insensitive response to Tamar's pain, and Tamar's pleading for a sensible resolution in marriage to her brother, as she knew that she now faced a life alone and rejected. What a sorrowful episode in the history of David's family, all likely set in place before any of these children of the king were twenty years old.

TO UNDERSTAND

Sexual abuse. Somebody (probably older or more powerful) made sexual contact with you. It may have been intercourse, oral sex, anal sex, simulated intercourse (using an object), touching or fondling parts of the body which are covered by a bathing suit, requiring the other to touch those same areas of the body, exposing the genitals, being seen naked, sexual kissing, being solicited for sexual purposes, exposure to por-nography, and being forced to observe others having sex. This is sexual abuse. Add to this list rape by an acquaintance or a stranger, date rape, or sexual involvement when your judgment was impaired by alcohol or drugs, as well as intercourse against your will in marriage. This is sexual assault, an additional expression of sexual abuse.

How do you feel when you read that list? Dirty, disgusted, sorrowful, livid? In your journal, write out a handful of the most descriptive words or images you can that describe feelings generated by this extensive list.

Who? Your abuser may have been a father, step-father, brother or uncle. It could have been your mother or aunt, because women sometimes sexually abuse children, though not nearly as often as men do. It often is someone you know, not a stranger. It could have been a teacher, pastor, coach or neighbor. You cannot tell by looking at someone if they are an abuser – or if they too have been sexually abused.

Pattern. There is often a pattern to what happens in child sexual abuse. At first, the one whose intention is to harm begins to cultivate a relationship with the child. There may be secrecy surrounding the relationship. Then, the abuser begins to make physical contact which appears to be OK. He may hold the child's hand, kiss, hug, hold her on his lap or rub her back. Then, over time (from a few minutes to months), the abuser makes sexual contact.

Sometimes the sexual abuse only occurs once, but often there is a continued abuse, either on a regular basis or intermittently. And after the initial contact, there are often threats or promises made to maintain the abuse and the secrecy surrounding it.

YOUR STORY

What happened to you? Are you ready to tell your story? When you are ready, it is helpful to your healing to speak the words out loud to someone you can trust, whether a counselor, friend, or other group members. You don't need to feel rushed to speak, but silence and secrets can keep us bound.

Sexual abuse rips apart what is meant to be whole.

Sexual trauma stains what is designed to be pure.

Sexual assault imprints with evil what is intended to be holy.

In your journal, describe in one or two sentences what was ripped apart in you from your experience of abuse. Describe in one or two sentences what was stained in you from your experience of abuse. Describe in one or two sentences what was imprinted with evil in you from your experience of abuse.

ACTION VERBS

Show up ~ pay attention ~ tell the truth ~
~release the outcome~

Color. Take a blank sheet of paper. Choose one crayon whose color corresponds to your feelings right now. Draw what you need to draw today. Repeat this exercise on a different day with a new color.

View. Artists through the centuries have given a visual dimension to this story. Sara Kipfer has collected a number of Baroque art expressions of the rape of Tamar that can be found at www.sbl-site.org, in an article entitled *Love Turns to Hate: The Rape of Tamar in Baroque Art*. Beginning with Kipfer's collection, take time to look at the ways Tamar and Amnon have been depicted over the centuries. (There are actually two women named Tamar in the Old Testament – look for the one associated with Amnon, not Judah).

Create. Writing in Psalm 56:8, the Psalmist says: "You keep track of all my sorrows. You have collected all my tears in your bottle. You have recorded each one in your book." Using the image of the tear-filled bottle, create your own bottle for tears. Take an empty jar or bottle and prepare it to be a symbolic receptacle for the tears you may shed during these days. It may or may not have a lid. You may want to be able to see through it, or you may want it to be protected. Paste scripture verses on your bottle, or decorate it with beautiful images or sparkly jewels. Make it yours.

Mirror work. Sark is a woman who writes wonderful books for women, sometimes a bit wild, but with lots of helpful ideas. In *Transformation Soup*, she describes what she calls "mirror work." To do this, follow her directions:

Stare into a mirror for many moments without preparing to go somewhere, or see "how you look," or fix your hair, look at your skin, or put on makeup. See what you see. AS IS. I usually see sadness or resignation or rage or forced perkiness or signs of clenching, resisting, or avoiding. Sometimes I try to adjust the "mask," which appears to have slipped. Then I usually go deeper. I speak to myself in the mirror and say, How are you, really? Then, I usually begin to cry. I cry until the tears transform into something else.

Read the story of Joseph in Genesis 37-39, especially the encounter with Potiphar's wife in chapter 39. The word used for Tamar's garment is the same word used for Joseph's robe (in chapter 37). What are the similarities and differences in the stories? Did their gender make a difference? Think about their physical attractiveness, their attempt at persuasion, their powerlessness, their desire to speak from high moral ground, and their inability to convince the other of their destructive advances.

View. With a friend, watch the section on Tamar from the video *Shattered Silhouttes* by Naimi Imani Lett. Process the feelings you experience with your friend.

Meditate on Tamar's story. Give yourself permission to stop when you need to, for it may be an intense experience. Place yourself in the palace of the King. Feel the elasticity of the dough as you knead it. Smell the bread baking. Taste its flavor. Experience Amnon's eyes as they cover you with his lust. Feel his hands grab at you. Sense Tamar's shame. Allow Absalom's anger to cover you.

PRAYER

Suffering Saviour,
In your crucifixion, Lord Jesus, you have borne my pain.
You were betrayed by one you trusted,
who sold you out for a few pieces of silver.
You understand the depth of my sense of betrayal.
You were deserted by those you loved,
and you know what it is like to be abandoned.
You chose to give up your power in order to bring us to redemption,
and you experienced being powerless to stop the abuse,
so you know what it is like for an abused woman to lie powerless.
Stripped naked and exposed, you went to the cross.
You indeed were a man of sorrows, acquainted with grief.
I am so grateful for your willingness to take upon your body
both my wounds and my sin.
I am in awe of your love.
Comfort me, your cherished daughter, with the comfort
that can only come from one who has suffered unto death.

With a grateful spirit,
Amen.

FROM THE MENDER'S BASKET

Ah, Lord God!
Behold, you have made the heavens and the earth
by your great power and outstretched arm.
There is nothing too hard for you.
Jeremiah 32:17

The great challenge is living your wounds through instead of thinking them through. It is better to cry than to worry, better to feel your wounds deeply than to understand them, better to let them enter into your silence than talk about them. In your head you can analyze them, find their causes and consequences, and coin words to speak and write about them. But no final healing is likely to come from that source. You need to let your wounds go down into your heart.
Henri Nouwen

A bruised reed he will not break,
and a smoldering wick he will not snuff out.
In faithfulness he will bring forth justice.
Isaiah 42:3

NEW THREADS TO FOLLOW

The Wounded Heart: Hope for Adult Victims of Childhood Sexual Abuse, Dan Allender. This comprehensive treatment of the subject also has a workbook which can be used individually or by a group.

Film - *White Oleander* - weep for the little girl.

Film - *Forrest Gump* - innocence betrayed.

Song - Amy Grant and Tom Hemby, *Ask Me*.

We Were the Least of These: Reading the Bible with Survivors of Sexual Abuse, Elaine A. Heath - an exploration of biblical passages that speak to the needs of those who have been sexually abused.

4

A BRAIDED RAG RUG

When, as an adult, she allows these coping behaviors
to continue in a way that keeps her from deeply entering into
relationship with those she is called to love,
she is no longer simply "coping" in legitimate ways.
She is violating God's highest commandments.
Sin that is ignored or denied lingers like
an untreated infection.
Dan Allender, *The Wounded Heart*

TO REMEMBER

When I was in junior high, I learned to sew in Home Economics class. I really enjoyed it, and began to make many of my own clothes. I purchased a floral print fabric with rich purples, blues and greens, and created a pair of slacks from that fabric. Proud of what I had sewn with my own hands, I wanted to wear them to school to display what I had done.

At the time I completed them, girls couldn't wear pants to school, but within a few weeks, that rule changed and I finally got to wear those glorious pants. You can imagine my pride in what I had created. However, shortly after I got to school, I was called down to the principal's office and sent home, because apparently those pants did not fit within the acceptable limits of the new dress code.

Were they too tight, too flashy, too conspicuous? That detail of the story escapes me, and I'm not sure that I ever received an explanation at that time, but even as I tell it decades later, I can still feel the flush of shame I experienced that day. What did that do to my budding female heart? I wanted to throw those pants in the rag bin, for they had become stained with my shame, even as innocent as my actions had been.

TAMAR'S STORY LINE.

As we return to Tamar's story, we now focus on the interaction between Amnon and Tamar immediately following the rape, as Tamar makes one final attempt to salvage the consequences of Amnon's actions - for herself, for her brother, and for the extended family.

In this action, Amnon moves from love/lust to the rejection of the object of his supposed affection.

Tamar moves from her place as virgin princess to one of a ruined young woman, who desperately attempts to find a solution to the situation.

The text is certainly not ambiguous in its description of Amnon in verse 15. "Then Amnon hated her with intense hatred. In fact, he hated her more than he had loved her." His words to her were harsh – "get up and get out." Amnon, in his illusion of power and control, probably thought that Tamar would immediately follow his direction. Even when faced with Amnon's disdain, Tamar tries one more time to convince her brother, her rapist, to keep her.

"No!" she said to him. "Sending me away would be a greater wrong than what you have already done to me."

Initially, Tamar's attempt to find a mutually beneficial solution to the situation seems strange. Could she possibly be considering a life with Amnon? How bad could life outside the palace be when compared to spending the rest of her days with the one who so violently abused her? Was she possibly trying to save face for her brother? Or was she only thinking about her own future?

Yet for Tamar, it was not to be, for Amnon, too, takes action in response to her plea. The verbs that describe what he did are explicit: he hated, he refused, and he called his servant, ordering Tamar to be cast out of his chamber, a disgraced woman. By bolting the door against her, Amnon is quickly washing his hands of his sister. He's taken what he wanted and now he's done with her.

Note the way Amnon involves others in his sin against his sister – first, through Shimeah's plotting; next by involving his father to summon Tamar to his chamber, and then through his personal servant, doing the dirty work to get rid of the mess. Here is a man who thinks nothing of using others to get what he wants. It is evident that this involvement did open the door for others to protect Tamar, to stand up for what is right in the moment, but no one stood for justice, for righteousness. Only Tamar.

TO UNDERSTAND.

The aftermath of abuse. The image we will use in this section is that of a braided rag rug, symbolic of our attempt to either fix ourselves on our own or to braid the stained piece into the rest of our life so that its damage can't be seen any longer. The comparison is fitting for what happens when we try to "just get on with life." At times we get all knotted up, and also are in danger of being stepped on.

Abuse is ugly. Abuse is sin. Abuse is life-changing. It damages the person who has been abused, and it forever alters the relational dynamics of the family of origin as well as the family that will one day be formed by the abused woman. The abused woman consequently may feel stained, torn – like the fabric in my gift-box of damaged remnants. So what do we do with these damaged scraps? Is there a way they can be salvaged? Restored? Redeemed?

How do we respond to abuse, to what has happened to us? What are our strategies for protecting ourselves, for taking matters into our own hands so we won't ever be hurt again? This chapter will reflect on the self-generated responses that come in three broad categories: our feelings, our thinking, and our behavior.

Feelings. A first response is our emotional reaction to the wounds we suffer, our feelings. These reactions seem to come naturally to us, and are important for us to acknowledge, attempt to understand, and learn from. Those emotions include the broad categories of sadness, fear, shame and anger.

Sadness, self-pity, pain, hurt. We are saddened by what has happened to us. It is a terrible loss. We were stripped of a portion of our childhood, an experience of adolescence which we deserved to have. As a child, we may not know why we sometimes feel sad, but as we become more aware of the impact of the abuse, we can better understand that loss. Sometimes, the pain we feel can cause us to try to medicate it with addictive substances or actions.

Fear. Depending upon the circumstances of our abuse, fear may have played a large role in our reactions. When the door-knob began to turn, when your drunken husband grabbed your arm, or when your neighbor turned the car off the road into a deserted lane, fear was your companion. Fear doesn't leave us when the abuse in finished, for it stands as a barrier between us and the danger of being hurt again. Fear may cause us to gain a lot of weight, to deny our femininity, to choose a partner who will not ask for our heart, or to stay stuck.

Where has fear "got your number?" In what area(s) of your life do you experience terror?

Shame. Shame over sin we've committed or over damage we've caused to another is considered legitimate shame. Shame is illegitimate when we hold ourselves responsible for the mess we are in and we loathe who we are. As painful as being hurt and rejected are, an explanation can be found to make sense of why we aren't loved as deeply as we desire: we are defective. We feel humiliated or embarrassed not so much about what we've done, but about who we are. The shame that surrounds sexual abuse may involve our unease with our sexuality, feelings of being used and dirty, the urge to take responsibility for another's actions that we don't need to own, or our desire to be incessantly loved.

To experience the essence of shame, think of something that happened to you that was of little importance as far as substance (not life-threatening, for example), but that was terribly humiliating (vomiting in public, being exposed in some way, walking in on someone having sex or using the bathroom, etc.). As you remember the scene, can you feel the shame in your body? What are you feeling? Where in your body is the shame making its presence known?

What are the areas of your life where shame continues to play out as a result of your abuse?

Anger. While anger may not be our first reaction, when the fog begins to lift, either in the weeks and months after the abuse or even as an adult, we become aware of our feelings of anger. It may exhibit itself in uncontrolled outbursts of rage, or it may turn inward into depression. We are angry at the abuser for what he did. We are angry at ourselves for being so gullible, so afraid, so needy, so stupid, so wanting. We are angry at our bodies for even a faint hint of response, and we are angry at our hearts for our hunger for relationship. We are angry at the adults in our lives for their failure to protect us. We are angry at God for letting it happen to us.

How does your anger play out? Who is it focused on?

Is it turned outward or turned inward?

61

Thoughts. A second way we deal with our experience of abuse is in our thinking. As a child, our first reaction to what happened is often confusion. *What has happened? Is it wrong? My "friend"(abuser) told me this was good, but it doesn't feel good.*

The sense of confusion is often accompanied by denial. We deny that it happened, we deny its severity, we deny that it really mattered, or we deny that we've been hurt by the sexual abuse. At times our denial takes the form of what psychologists call dissociation, a detachment from reality when we find ourselves somehow removed from our bodies in order to protect our heart. This can be as simple as day-dreaming, or as serious as the loss of identity or memory found in some dissociative disorders.

Another response is to go to the place of *stinkin' thinkin,'* in which we paint our life with a negative paintbrush, allowing our self-talk, the voice that has a conversation with us throughout the day, to control what we're thinking. This can come in a number of categories as David Burns suggests:

- ➤ All-or-nothing thinking
- ➤ Overgeneralization
- ➤ Mental filter
- ➤ Discounting the positive
- ➤ Jumping to conclusions

➤ Magnifying the importance of your problems and short-comings

➤ Emotional reasoning

➤ "Should" statements

➤ Labeling – "I made a mistake" becomes "I'm a loser"

➤ Personalization and blame

This kind of thinking involves the following self-talk comments. Add your own to the list.

➤ I am flawed.

➤ I am worthless.

➤ I am ugly.

➤ I am to blame.

➤ I won't amount to anything.

➤ I have to pay.

➤ I can't love.

➤ I don't matter.

➤ I don't deserve to be loved.

Actions. When we think and feel in certain ways, then we have to choose behaviors, by intentional choice or by default, to cope with those thoughts and feelings. We most often respond to our abuse by determining to get away, give in or get even. As a child, we may have done our best to get away, to figure out ways to make ourselves invisible to our abuser, or to avoid being alone or being accessible to another person.

A second response is to give in, to let what is inevitable happen. Some reports of abuse talk about the child watching his/her own abuse as if they are looking down from the ceiling or are huddled across the room, giving in physically but distancing themselves emotionally.

In a third response, children sometimes fantasize as to how they might get even with their attacker, often based on magical thinking or scenarios from a television drama.

As adults, these types of reactions continue to be present in our lives, becoming common reactions to all kinds of situations. One of these may become our typical pattern of response, or we may bounce around all three. Think about your actions over the past week. In what ways did you attempt to get away? In what ways did you give in? In what ways did you try to get even? Which of the three is your most common response?

YOUR STORY

Feelings. There have been many questions for you to ponder already about your feelings in regards to your abuse. Just remember – no emotions are bad in themselves. Whether we're mad, glad, sad or scared – or anywhere in between – we can accept our emotions as our own, and honor their integrity.

Thoughts. Hear the Word of the Lord as it stands up to the lies of our negative thinking.

I am worthless: *So don't be afraid; you are worth more than many sparrows.* Matthew 10:31

I am an orphan: *Yet to all who received him, to those who believed in his name, he gave the right to become children of God.* John 1:12

I am ugly: *For we are God's workmanship, created in Christ Jesus to do good works, which God prepared in advance for us to do.* Ephesians 2:10

I am to blame: *Therefore, there is now no condemnation for those who are in Christ Jesus.* Romans 8:1

I won't amount to anything: *"For I know the plans I have for you," declares the Lord, "plans to prosper you and not to harm you, plans to give you hope and a future."* Jeremiah 29:11

I have to pay: *Therefore, since we have been justified through faith, we have peace with God through our Lord Jesus Christ.* Romans 5:1

I am bound: *You will know the truth, and the truth will set you free.* John 8:32.

I don't deserve to be loved: *I have loved you with an everlasting love.* Jeremiah 31:3

Memorize a scripture verse from those noted above to combat those thoughts when they come.

Actions When the temptation to get away, give in or get even comes our way, we do have alternate reactions. Instead of getting away, we can stay engaged. Instead of giving in, we can stand our ground. Instead of getting even, we can move on. Remember - the one who seeks revenge digs two graves.

ACTION VERBS

~Show up ~ pay attention ~ tell the truth ~
~release the outcome~

Create. Write or draw a picture of one time in the last week when you gave into *stinkin' thinkin.'*

Pray. As much as prayer needs to be an integral part of our lives at any time, during this time of focus on healing from sexual abuse, it can be helpful to pray in a specific way with a counselor, spiritual director, or close friend.

Counselor Morven Baker suggests a simple pattern of prayer that asks Jesus to take us to a safe place as we approach the memories of abuse. It begins with shutting the eyes, centering the self, and quieting the voices that often bombard us. Then, we ask Jesus to take us to a safe place, a place where we can hear his voice. We invite Jesus to be present in the time, in the place of our abuse, and we gently sit in that space as we remember, asking Jesus to take us to him in these quiet moments. As we pray, we can be open to feel the touch of Jesus, to hear words of comfort, to see the tears in Jesus' eyes.

Record your thoughts and reactions following this period of prayer in your journal pages.

Create. Carlene Hacker describes shame as "like a sly creature who sneaks in from behind and slithers between my feelings, spreading long, transparent tentacles over my eyes." Draw or paint picture or form a word image of what that "sly creature" looks like.

View. Watch the movie *Good Will Hunting*. When it comes to

67

the part in which Robin Williams pleads with Will to believe that "it's not your fault," rewind the movie and watch the scene again. After doing so, make a list of the ways you've assumed some unwarranted blame in connection with your abuse or assault, and then write the true statement next to it. Across each of the false statements, write in large letters: IT'S NOT MY FAULT.

Here's an example of a faulty belief: I was raped because I wore a skimpy top.

Here is the truth: I was raped because my attacker was out of control and chose not to control his actions. IT WASN'T MY FAULT!

Create. Using magazines or newspapers, make a stinkin' thinkin' collage. Find or compose sentences that are untrue. As you paste each phrase on the collage, speak a positive statement out loud in opposition to each negative one.

Meditate on the story of the woman with an issue of blood found in Mark 5:21-34. Put yourself in her place. Feel her body, feel the lifeblood dripping out of her day after day. Feel the shame of that experience, especially of being unclean in the eyes of the religious leaders. Experience the crowds around her, jostling her back and forth, even as she tried not to touch them. Smell the sweat of the men. Hear Jesus' voice, always teaching. Reach out her hand to grab the hem of his garment. Feel the coarse fabric brush your fingers. Watch him turn around, and hear the words, "who touched me?" Feel the flush of shame at being exposed turn to gratitude when the healing power coursed through her body. Consider the question - are you willing to reach your hand out to touch his robe?

PRAYER

Jehovah-Rapha, the one who mends,
Peel off the layers of bandages I have applied to
staunch the shameful hemorrhage of my soul.
Probe the wounds that continue to fester;
cleanse them deeply, gently, thoroughly.

I open to your healing touch the wound of sadness and self-pity,
the hurt and the pain I have suffered.
Ease the ache.
I seek your forgiveness for the pity parties I've hosted on my own behalf
in my willingness to stay in the mess of my life.
I ask your direction as I seek after a godly sorrow over sin,
both mine and that of another.

I open to your healing power the wound of fear.
I claim the perfect love that promises to cast out all fear.
Remove the sense of terror from my dreams, from flashbacks, and replace
the terror with an assurance of your peace.
Give me the wisdom to know how best to be as wise as a serpent, but as
innocent as a dove.

I open to your healing light the wound of shame.
Restore a sense of your created dignity within me.
Relieve me of the responsibility of another's sin.

I open to your healing presence the wound of anger.
I seek your forgiveness for the ways in which I have hurt others through
the daggers of words and piercing looks I have tossed at them.
Enable me to own my anger, and to grieve over the sin which angers you.
Allow me to be angry without sinning against another.

Pour out your healing ointment.
Bring me to the healing balm of Gilead.
In the name of the wounded healer,
Amen.

THE MENDER'S BASKET

They dress the wound of my people
as though it were not serious.
"Peace, peace," they say,
when there is no peace.
Are they ashamed of their loathsome conduct?
They do not even know how to blush.
Jeremiah 6:14-15

Jesus meets each individual
at his or her point of intense shame.
Margaret Alter, *Resurrection Psychology*

Though we have come to believe in Christ
and have grown into a deep conviction of faith,
there is still one place sealed off,
one place where healing is not allowed,
one place where we shy away from complete openness.
So if to trust involves opening up,
if to believe means laying ourselves open,
if to love is to make ourselves vulnerable,
then rather than taking the risk of faith,
we choose to doubt.
Os Guinness, *God in the Dark*

The woman recovering from abuse or other stressful life situations may feel she's in no way in charge of anything, least of all her own world. She faces the horse with trepidation. The horse senses the fear and becomes tense and concerned. The wise instructor starts small. The woman is handed a soft brush and sent to fuss over the horse. It's pointed out that if she stands close to the animal, she will be out of range of a well-aimed kick. She is warned to watch for tell-tale signs of fear in herself and the horse. She's warned to keep her feet out from under the horse's stomping hoof. They're both allowed to back away and regroup and try again until they reach an accord regarding personal space. Calm prevails, and within a few minutes, hours or sessions, interaction becomes friendship. It happens almost every time a woman is allowed enough time and space to work through the situation.

Joanne M. Friedman, *Horses in the Yard*

If anyone builds on this foundation using
gold, silver, costly stones, wood, hay or straw,
their work will be shown for what it is,
because the day will bring it to light.
I Corinthians 3:12

We are all wounded.
But wounds are necessary for his healing light
to enter into our beings.
Without wounds and failure and frustrations and defeats,
there will be no opening for his brilliance
to trickle in and invade our lives.
Failures in life are courses with very high tuition fees,
so I don't cut classes and miss my lessons:
on humility,
on patience,
on hope,
on asking others for help,
on listening to God,
on trying again and again and again.
Bo Sanchez, *You Have The Power to Create Love*

NEW THREADS TO FOLLOW

Inside Out, Larry Crabb - a classic on looking beyond outward appearances.

The Healing Path, Dan Allender - Allender continues the journey with us.

Wounds that Heal, Stephen Seamands - a look at the suffering of the cross.

"The Top 10 Types of "Stinkin' Thinkin."" David Burns. *Psych Central.* http://psychcentral.com/lib/2006/the-top-10-types-of-stinkin-thinkin/

5

A PATCHWORK QUILT

Hope begins when the memory of what was
becomes a longing for what is to be restored
Jan Meyers, *The Allure of Hope*

TO REMEMBER.

There is a touching scene near the end of the movie *Stepmom* in which the dying mother creates a quilt for her daughter out of pieces of fabric symbolic of the girl's life.

As I think of the fabrics that would make up a similar healing quilt of my life, a comforter to bring warmth and protection, I begin with the fabrics of precious memory. These include the pale yellow dotted Swiss that I carefully crafted into my prom gown, the red velveteen of the party dress my father bought for me, the navy and gold wool of the suit I wore for my first professional conference presentation, and the silk of the nightgown my baby caressed as he nursed at my breast.

Some of the fabrics for my quilt come with ambivalence: the navy blue serge of my first Salvation Army uniform, symbolic of the tensions between the constrictions of its culture and the ministry opportunities it offered, the fluorescent orange of the mini-dress I made in 10th grade, as I was trying to discover my identity, and the lace of my wedding gown, sewn with such high expectations, yet quickly bringing me face to face with the reality of marriage and family.

I must also make room to hold and embrace the painful swatches. The brilliant purples, blues and greens of the forbidden pants. The black corduroy of the torn jumper. The pattern of the cotton hospital gown when I miscarried our longed-for baby. The red sweater I wore the first time I was abused.

In spite of the pain, I must carefully add each fragment of these fabrics to my quilt, allowing Jehovah-Rapha to stitch them together seamlessly, removing the shame and replacing it with grace.

Ruth Ray and Susan McFadden provide some thoughts on the quilt as a metaphor for spiritual development as well as emotional healing.

> A quilt has multiple layers and is crafted over time. Like the individual differences found in ways of being spiritual, some people's quilts have an organizing structure immediately apparent to all; others are of the "crazy quilt" variety that, when viewed partially may make little sense, but can be quite beautiful when seen as a whole.

Quilts, like spirituality, may have different functions at different points in the life span. Sometimes, they are folded up and put away, with only a part of their pattern showing; at other times, they are used daily for warmth and security.

A very important aspect of quilt making is that although parts of the quilt (its "blocks") may be crafted individually, the whole quilt is traditionally the outcome of people gathering to stitch it together. Most of the time, the intricate stitching patterns are actually quite hard to see unless one inspects the quilt closely. As spirituality is nurtured across the life span through relationships with others, the "stitches" of those relational encounters may be quite hard to distinguish when viewed in the context of the whole pattern of life. Nevertheless, without them, there could be no holistic, integrated sense of spirituality.

Taking the metaphor just a bit further, historically women gathered to create quilts for their families to use and pass along to other generations; groups of women have also dedicated considerable time to making quilts for strangers in need. Both of these activities—caring for one's family and caring for strangers—are important aspects of spiritual development that are not obvious in metaphors of individual heroic journeys.

See the Ray and McFadden reference in the New Threads to Follow section for more thoughts on the quilt as a metaphor for spiritual formation and healing.

TAMAR'S STORY LINE

Tamar has been unsuccessful in her desperate attempt to persuade Amnon to stay with her, so now Tamar acts. As she leaves the place of her rape and of her life as she has known it, she doesn't go quietly. She was not willing to keep the abuse a secret.

When she entered her brother's chamber, she was wearing a richly ornamented robe, for this was the kind of garment the virgin daughters of the king wore. The scripture is explicit in verse 16: "Tamar put ashes on her head and tore the ornamented robe she was wearing. She put her hands on her head and went away, weeping aloud as she went."

The symbolism of her actions is important to note. In her actions, Tamar openly expressed her grief and distress, publicly demonstrated her change in position (tearing of the robe), and made sure that her plight was known, allowing Amnon's sin against her to be recognized by others.

How did Tamar remember that horrible day? Did she realize that she did what was within her power to resist Amnon's attack? As Pamela Cooper-White suggests, did Tamar recognize that she had no power over her brother or the other men of the story, but that she did have "power-within," an *en-theos* (God-within) to speak up, to suggest alternatives to violence and banishment?

What were the rest of her days like? What was triggered in her when she smelled the aroma of baking bread? When she dressed in the dull-colored clothing of a non-virgin? When she dreamed of the marriage that was no longer possible?

Enter Absalom into the narrative. Now he shows up. Now he will get involved, but on his own terms. In his own time.

How did it feel to hear Absalom's words to his sister, "don't take this thing to heart"? Do you think he was diminishing the extent of the attack, or suggesting that she shouldn't worry, that he was going to take care of it? Was Absalom more concerned about saving the family's "face" than acknowledging the damage to his sister's life?

Has anyone said something like that to you? If so, take time in your journal to describe what happened and how you felt.

"When King David heard this, he was furious." Well, it's about time! Yet even in his anger, there is no record of David's actions. Come on, Dad. Your teen-age daughter has just been raped by her brother. Do something. Take her to her mother. Don't leave her desolate in her brother's house. Do something to punish Amnon. Just do something.

The inaction displayed by David is all too common in cases of incest. In the desire to preserve some semblance of family honor and reputation, the daughter is sent away, is disbelieved, is cast aside. Indeed, Solomon, another of David's sons, got it right – there is nothing new under the sun.

What we discover as we read further into the book of 2nd Samuel is that the consequences of Amnon's act were far-reaching. Tamar did not remain silent. Absalom moved from brother to vengeful protector. David, although furious, did not intervene. Tamar's mother is still unseen. Absalom affects revenge. Amnon loses his life. David grieves for Amnon, and banishes Absalom, virtually losing two sons at the same time. The course of history is changed forever and Solomon, not Amnon or Absalom, ultimately becomes king of Israel. End of Act Three

TO UNDERSTAND

Healing work As we bring the swatches representing our lives to our Mender, Jehovah-Rapha, it is with the belief that truly, all things work together for good. Hear how novelist Susan Howatch describes this in *High Flyer*:

Your new life - which will benefit not just you but those you meet - will be shaped by your new knowledge, the knowledge which has arisen directly out of the suffering you've had to endure. All things can be worked by God into his creative purposes . . . and there's no darkness so dark that in the end it can't be penetrated and subsumed by the light . . . but remember, you must act.

Four truths. As we act, there are four truths for us to remember:

The first is that **healing takes time**. When we least expect it, there are periods in which God intervenes and allows for rapid growth in us. However, in the same way there are other phases when it is slow going and we wonder if we've hit a wall, if we're headed back to Shur. It is in those times that we must be patient, grateful for the baby steps we've been able to make toward wholeness.

Pause now and write out three baby steps (or giant steps) that you've taken over the last month that reflect God's healing work in your life.

Example: last week, on the way to church, I was able to hold back sarcastic words that would have shamed my husband.

Recognize, too, that **healing is painful** at times. Using the quilting metaphor, some pieces of fabric need to be cut or trimmed, and some discarded. They also need to be basted into place before the final quilting is done. So too with our work of examining, praying, changing, trying out new roles, and reaching for new vision. It may be painful, but it is worth the risk.

We also must accept the truth that **healing is never finished.** Complete healing will not be ours until heaven. We have been forever changed by our life experience, and we will always have scars even when healing has taken place.

The fourth is that there are **no one-size-fits-all patterns** to this path of healing. Some additional resources are included in the Threads to Follow section, but there are no guarantees or quick fixes in this process. The joy of our spiritual quilt-making is that each is unique. So keep your thimbles on, and catch a vision of what a healing change could look like in your life in the various categories we've been looking at through these pages.

Feelings As our feelings are redeemed, self-pity and sadness move deeper into godly sorrow. "Sorrow begins to melt the victim's callused hatred toward herself and others," suggests

84

Dan Allender in *The Wounded Heart*. We come to mourn, to grieve the losses we have faced.

Make a list of significant losses you have experienced in your life. Spend time praying over that list, asking the Lord to reveal those areas which are still tender. Consider where you are in the process described by Kubler-Ross of denial, anger, bargaining, depression and acceptance. If you are stuck on one of those levels, it may be helpful to seek some assistance in coming to grips with the grief you are feeling.

Write one statement about how self-pity has been exposed in your life in recent days.

What is one step you can take this week to intentionally welcome the experience of godly sorrow?

Fear as the first reaction (the default setting) will begin to yield to courage. Think of how young children who live in fear react. They automatically cringe. Like small children, we've developed "cringe reflexes" that come automatically in response to certain triggers. As healing comes to us, we begin to recognize these reflexes, and refuse to allow them to rule us.

Write one statement about how fear has been apparent in your life.

What is one step you can take this week to intentionally take courage?

Shame seeks out appropriate responsibility for our own sin but also begins to move toward grace as we offer forgiveness to ourselves. We begin to be able to tell the difference between what someone has done to us that humiliates or shames us, and what we do with what has happened to us. We refuse to accept responsibility for another's sin toward us. We are able to hold our head up, and speak out what is true.

Write one statement about how shame has been exposed in your life.

What is one step you can take this week to intentionally move away from shame?

Rage transforms over time into a passion for justice and a desire to offer grace to another. Anger turned inward or directed outward begins to decrease, while outrage over injustice grows within us. It may lead us to a ministry that grows out of our own pain, as the place of humiliation and shame transforms into a source of spiritual authority within us.

Write one statement about how rage is being tempered in your life.

What is one step you can take this week to intentionally move toward a passion for justice?

Thoughts. As we move towards healing and wholeness, denial is exposed and is replaced by a recognition and acceptance of the truth.

Write three statements of truth about your history. Example: "I have been abused, and my gentle spirit has been damaged by the abuse."

Write one statement about how denial has been exposed in your life.

What is one step you can take this week to intentionally move toward truth?

Negative, *stinkin' thinkin'* is discarded, and replaced by the truths of the gospel.

Write one statement about how you have battled *stinkin' thinkin'* in your life and replaced it with positive thinking.

What is one step you can take this week to intentionally move toward positive thinking?

Behavior As we move toward wholeness, we no longer need

to depend upon the self-protective strategies we have used to give us the illusion of safety.

Instead of trying to get away, we work to stay in the moment, in the relationship.

What might that look like for you?

Instead of always giving in, we stand firm.

What might that look like for you?

Instead of getting even in our relationships, we offer a second chance, we turn the other cheek, we forgive.

What might that look like for you?

YOUR STORY

As we fashion our new quilt, the tattered rags which we so clumsily tried to braid together are offered for transformation. Pray specifically as you lift up the rags in each area to the Mender. Ask for the Serenity Prayer's serenity, courage, and wisdom.

God, give me grace to accept with serenity
the things that cannot be changed,
Courage to change the things

which should be changed,
and the Wisdom to distinguish
the one from the other.
Living one day at a time,
Enjoying one moment at a time,
Accepting hardship as a pathway to peace,
Taking, as Jesus did,
This sinful world as it is,
Not as I would have it,
Trusting that You will make all things right,
If I surrender to Your will,
So that I may be reasonably happy in this life,
And supremely happy with You forever in the next.
Amen.

Rudolph Niebuhr

ACTION VERBS

~Show up ~ pay attention ~ tell the truth ~
~release the outcome~

View. Watch the movie Stepmom. Near the end, the mother makes a quilt for her daughter, which is created from clothing which has a symbolic meaning for her. Consider how you might do that for yourself. It may actually be a quilt, or a wall hanging. It could be a collage or a notebook in which you write about each fabric. Try to choose pieces which have a mixture of emotions tied to them. As you create the quilt, either from the actual fabric or from similar fabric, paper, words, etc., touch each fabric carefully. Remind yourself of its story. Allow Jehovah-Rapha to heal the memories from those swatches which bring you pain. Acknowledge the fabrics that symbolize ambivalence, and pray for the willingness to live in that tension. Celebrate the memories which bring you joy, perhaps even touching base with someone who shared that joy with you.

Quilt. Create a word quilt. Find a simple pattern for a quilt square or block and print it out in black and white. Look through the previous chapters of this book as well as your journal and fill the shapes with the hard words, the painful words you find on its pages. Then take markers, paint, or whatever other medium you choose and cover these words with words and images of grace, peace, intimacy, faith, creativity, love, joy, and beauty. Use your creativity.

Research the story of the AIDS quilt on the Internet. You can start at www.aidsquilt.org. If there was a community quilt for sexual abuse and assault victims, how would the design of your square reflect your life and your vision for the future? Draw it out or create a fabric square.

Bake homemade bread, using your hands to knead the dough and your oven to bake the bread – no need to use a bread machine today. Remember Tamar's story, how she formed the bread for her brother out of a good heart toward him. Use all of your senses. Enjoy the texture of the dough, the work of your hands. Catch yourself humming a song of praise as you knead the dough. Breathe deeply in the scent of the yeast, the aroma of baking bread. Gaze with a glimmer of joy at the rising of the dough and at the golden crust of the finished loaf. Finally, taste the baked bread, hot and fresh from your own hands, your own oven. Lick the strawberry jam off your fingers. Enjoy the simple pleasure of the redeemed bread (with thanks to Elaine Heath for the idea in *We Were the Least of These*).

Create a word picture of yourself as a whole and holy woman, healed and forgiven. Choose to use an essay format or poetry, or simply make a list of words. Consider what might need to be repented of in order for that picture to be completed. Consider what healing you may need to pray for in order for that picture to be completed. Consider what root of bitterness needs to be exposed and offered to Jehovah-Rapha in order for that picture to be completed. Do what the Spirit of Jehovah-Rapha is calling you to do.

Listen to Kim Hill's recording of "Holy, You Are Still Holy." Create your own expression of dance or other worship unto the Lord as the music plays.

Meditate. Find an image that speaks to you of the care of the Lord for you and meditate upon it. Suggested themes to look for are ways in which God is depicted as a comforting mother, a shelter in the rock, an eagle protecting its young, a shepherd, etc.

PRAYER

Master Designer,
You who created the heavens and the earth,
who sprinkled the ink of darkness with the stars of the universe,
do your re-creative work in me.
I offer you these meager patches of fabric, and I place them in your
hands, trusting you to handle them gently.
Piece together these fragile fragments, one by one,
tenderly basting their stories in place upon my heart.
Shine your penetrating light upon each memory, as you connect the dis-
jointed swatches with your healing power.
Let me wait upon you to do your mending work
within me and through me.
Yet as I wait, allow me to catch a glimpse of the
whole, healed woman you desire me to be in Christ.
Through this exciting yet difficult journey,
I pray that I might receive your protective covering over me,
so that I might have the strength and courage to take today's
step of faith.
You, indeed, are my King,
Amen.

THE MENDER'S BASKET

There is a place of quiet rest, near to the heart of God.
A place where sin cannot molest, near to the heart of God.
O Jesus, blest redeemer, sent from the heart of God.
Hold us who wait before thee, near to the heart of God.
Cleland McAfee

For you did not receive the spirit of bondage again to fear, but you received the Spirit of adoption by whom we cry out, "Abba, Father."
Romans 8:15 (NKJV)

There is so much rejection, pain and woundedness among us,
but once you choose to claim the joy hidden in the midst of
all suffering, life becomes a celebration. Joy never denies the
sadness but transforms it to a fertile soil for more joy.
Henri Nouwen

He who began a good work in you will be faithful to complete it.
Philippians 1:6

The wound is the place where the Light enters you.
Rumi

There is a balm in Gilead to make the wounded whole,
There is a balm in Gilead to heal the sin-sick soul.
Sometimes I feel discouraged and think my work's in vain,
But then the Holy Spirit revives my soul again.
There is a balm in Gilead to make the wounded whole,
There is a balm in Gilead to heal the sin-sick soul.
Traditional Spiritual (Jeremiah 8:22)

The emotion that can break your heart is sometimes the very
one that heals it . . .
Nicholas Sparks, *At First Sight*

It's like this old patchwork quilt my momma used to have . .
Each piece on that quilt meant something. And some of
those pieces were the damn ugliest things you've ever seen . .
But some of the pieces were so beautiful they almost hurt my
eyes to look at when I was a kid . . .That's the best you can
hope for, Danny. That your life turns out like that patchwork
quilt. That you can add some bright, sparkling pieces to the
dirty, stained ones you have so far. That in the end, the bright
patches might take up more space on your quilt than the dark
ones.
Brooke McKinley, *Shades of Gray*

NEW THREADS TO FOLLOW

Door of Hope: Recognizing and Resolving the Pains of Your Past, Jan Frank - a powerful story of restoration.

On the Threshold of Hope: Opening the Door to Healing for Survivors of Sexual Abuse, Diane Mandt Langberg - an excellent guide for survivors and for those who love them.

Story - "The Ragman," in the book *Ragman and Other Stories of Faith,* Walter Wangarin - a wonderful image of the redemption of rags.

Song - "Something Beautiful," Gloria Gaither - a song of hope.

Film - A Big Fish - the healing power of stories.

Shame and Grace, Lewis Smedes, and any of John Bradshaw's books for shame, for a fuller understanding of its power.

The Wounded Healer, Henri Nouwen - for the redemption of sorrow.

How to Make an American Quilt, a film that tells a story of family.

The Web and the Quilt: Alternatives to the Heroic Journey toward Spiritual Development. Ruth E. Ray and Susan F. McFadden. 2001. *Journal of Adult Development* 8, 4, 201-211.

6

AN EXQUISITE TAPESTRY

The Weaver will not be discouraged or deterred.
We weave a fabric which no one's violence will destroy,
and I discover the beauty of me.
Catherine J. Foote, *Survivor Prayers*

TO REMEMBER

When I had completed an early draft of Tamar's story, I invited a group of women connected to our ministry to join together weekly to work through the material I'd developed. Through my relationships with them, I knew that some had experienced sexual abuse personally, while others simply wanted to gain a better understanding of the topic of sexual abuse.

As we spent time with the scriptural narrative and interacted with our own stories, the Spirit of God was at work, revealing truth and providing comfort and healing. For one woman in particular, our time together brought her own teen-age memory of sexual abuse to light – a part of her story that she had never spoken aloud to anyone before.

We decided to conclude the group with a day-long retreat at the home of one of the participants. In our desire to provide a tangible reminder of that day to our sisters, Barb brought a cross with a thimble for each woman, while my penchant for bargain shopping had provided multihued sewing baskets for each one to take home.

That sewing basket was sitting on the kitchen table in the home of the woman whose own abuse had been unacknowledged for so many years. Her mother stopped by her home, and casually mentioned the basket. "Oh, I really like that sewing basket. Where did you get that?" "Well, mom, I've been meeting with a group of women and we received that as a reminder of our time together. Let me tell you what happened . . ."

I've discovered that the redemption provided by Jehovah-Rapha in the healing from sexual abuse comes in small, ordinary pieces and in glorious bursts of light. It comes as a woman picks up a basket and tells her story. It comes as I slip on a silky blouse whose bold patterns and brilliant purples, greens and blues are reminiscent of the forbidden pants. It comes in the gentle and sorrowful receiving of another's story of rape, of incest, of abuse as we sit quietly together. It comes in the candlelight vigil, as I stand shoulder to shoulder with sisters and brothers who pause to remember.

Redemption comes as I worship in God's house and hear the story of Tamar proclaimed. It comes as I tuck the quilt of

100

memory around my shoulders, resting in its gentle embrace. It comes as I cradle my newborn granddaughter, vowing to protect her with every breath that I have. And I trust that it will come when I hand these pages to a modern-day sister of Tamar, with the prayer that her story may be redeemed through her own courage and the touch of Jehovah-Rapha, the God who mends the broken.

TAMAR'S STORY LINE

And what of Tamar? Did redemption come for her? Was she able to discover, as Foote notes, "the beauty of me"? After the attack, Tamar is described as being a desolate woman. This word is used in other places in the Old Testament as being destroyed by an enemy, being torn to pieces by an animal, or describing land that is plundered, raped or destroyed. What is your own definition/word picture of the word desolate in regards to the aftermath of your abuse?

Was there anyone in the palace who loved Tamar?

Did a caring woman come alongside her?

Did she find healing?

Did her desolation bring her weeping for a night, but joy in the morning, the words of her father as recorded in Psalm 30?

Was her father's God Jehovah-Rapha to Tamar?

Life goes on. Even for Tamar, life went on. The little information we have about Tamar at the end of her story allows us to use our imagination to see what might have been. We know nothing more about what happened to her, for the last mention of her is as a desolate woman in the house of Absalom. However, we are given one further glimpse in II Samuel 14:27: "Three sons and a daughter were born to Absalom. The daughter's name was Tamar, and she became a beautiful woman."

In this child, we see the hope of redemption. In *Texts of Terror*, Phyllis Trible suggests that "In her (the child Tamar) Absalom has created a living memorial for his sister . . . from aunt to niece have passed name and beauty, so that rape and desolation have not the final word in the story of Tamar."

Tamar's abuse was not only redeemed through her beautiful niece; it was also redeemed in her voice that speaks through the centuries. Think about these questions. First, how was this story known? The only way that anyone could have known what was said in that bedchamber was if either Amnon or Tamar repeated it to someone. Maybe Amnon did tell the story, but it seems more likely to me that Tamar spoke the words of her story to another, who ultimately told them to the narrator of the story.

The telling of her story comes first in her actions, as she put

102

ashes on her head, tore her ornamented robe, put her hands on her head, and wept loudly, publicly. Her actions became a statement of accusation to her brother, and were likely understood in her culture as clearly as if she was standing on the street corner, holding up a sign for all to see.

Was there a further exchange of words between Absalom and Tamar? The narrator only records Absalom's words, as unsatisfying as they are to Tamar and to the contemporary reader. Did she speak words of explanation to her brother, or was Amnon's character so well known that Absalom assumed the worst the moment he saw his sister's grief?

And how did David hear about this? Did Tamar speak the words to her father, or did she go to Maacah for comfort, expecting her mother to speak to her father of her assault? Or perhaps it was Absalom who told David. We don't know, but what we do know is that David was furious but did nothing.

So here's the other question. Why is this story recorded in such detail in the scriptures? How did this account of rape make it to The Book? The simple answer is that God wanted it there. Elohei Mishpat, the God of justice, needed the story to be recorded. Jehovah-Rapha, the God of healing, the God of mercy, needed the story to be remembered and redeemed.

TO UNDERSTAND

You see, when weaving a blanket, an Indian woman leaves a
flaw in the weaving of that blanket to let the soul out.
Martha Graham

Life goes on for us as well, just as it did for Tamar. We live in a time where the terror and toll of sexual abuse is better understood than in the days of Tamar, and there is support available within the body of Christ and in the professional mental health field so that abuse, rape and desolation do not have the final word in our stories. I am trusting that during your journey in these pages, as well as in the counseling office, Jehovah-Rapha has come alongside, has touched you, and is mending your fragile offerings.

As healing comes, we begin to live more and more out of a heart of gratitude. We find ourselves longing to worship, to praise and to serve others. We feel a connection with other women, with Tamar, with unnamed women through the centuries and in the house around the corner. We watch with anticipation as threads of our story are interwoven with those of another, and another, and another. An exquisite tapestry is being created, still with its knots and tangles, but reflecting a glorious image of Rapha's healing touch, Christ's redemptive sacrifice, and the Comforter's empowering presence.

YOUR STORY

So what now? Whether through the pages of this book, in conversation with a trusted spiritual companion, or in a season of professional counseling, the time comes to step over our wounds, to develop an identity that goes beyond victim. Like the scars from a burn, the abuse will always be with us, but with time and care, hard work and determination, they can fade into the background of our lives.

ACTION VERBS

~ Show up ~ pay attention ~ tell the truth ~
~ release the outcome ~

Share. Remember the bread you baked at the end of the last chapter? Bake a loaf of bread to give to someone else. It may be for one who has walked the path with you, or for someone who you know is hurting just now. It may be for an acquaintance that you want to know better, or for someone whose story parallels yours. As you share the bread with them, tell of God's weaving, mending presence in your life.

Walk. Walk prayerfully on a deserted beach, on a path in the woods, or in your neighborhood or city at sunrise. Choose a shell, a piece of wood, a flower, or a stone or rock to bring home with you as a symbol of the work you've done, as a symbol of gratitude.

Celebrate. Read these words from Catherine J. Foote, writing in *Survivor Prayers:*

I celebrate a mother God, gently weaving, working carefully.
I celebrate the hands of skill, creating beauty within me.
I celebrate the working of the loom, reconnecting myself,
weaving a tapestry that picks up threads of
pain and anger and grief and loss,
and power and courage and strength and grace.

Chose some kind of ritual to mark the work you have done in these pages. Share a meal with the companion who has walked this path with you. Release a balloon. Write a letter to your abuser and then burn it. Thrown stones into the river. Go down to the river to pray. Share in the bread and wine of the Eucharist.

Create a work of art to celebrate your steps in recovery.

Speak. Find a way to tell your story. Share it with a trusted friend. Tell your mother or daughter. Give a testimony at a group meeting or as part of a worship service (with respect for the children who may be there). Speak at a symposium on child abuse. Speak to the legislature. Write about your experience on your blog. Find a way to use words to describe your healing.

Stand. Get involved in your community in regards to sexual abuse, domestic violence and/or child abuse. Wear a wristband. Attend a candlelight vigil. Stand with others who have suffered. Pray. Discover more about human trafficking on an international basis. Get involved.

Write a story or poem about Tamar as an old woman, or draw a picture of her. Dream of who she might have become if those around her loved her and supported her.

FROM THE MENDER'S BASKET

Wounding and healing are not opposites. They're part of the same thing. It is our wounds that enable us to be compassionate with the wounds of others. It is our limitations that make us kind to the limitations of other people. It is our loneliness that helps us to find other people or to even know they're alone with an illness. I think I have served people perfectly with parts of myself I used to be ashamed of.
Rachel Naomi Remen

If no one remembers a misdeed or names it publicly, it remains invisible. To the observer, its victim is not a victim and its perpetrator is not a perpetrator; both are misperceived because the suffering of the one and the violence of the other go unseen. A double injustice occurs – the first when the original deed is done and the second when it disappears.
Miroslav Volf

It has been said, 'time heals all wounds.'
I do not agree. The wounds remain.
In time, the mind, protecting its sanity, covers them with scar tissue and the pain lessens.
But it is never gone.
Rose Kennedy

In a futile attempt to erase our past, we deprive the community of our healing gift. If we conceal our wounds out of fear and shame, our inner darkness can neither be illuminated nor become a light for others.

Brennan Manning,

Abba's Child: The Cry of the Heart for Intimate Belonging

Destiny itself is like a wonderful wide tapestry in which every thread is guided by an unspeakable tender hand, placed beside another thread and held and carried by a hundred others.

Rainer Maria Rilke

We have renounced secret and shameful ways;
we do not use deception,
nor do we distort the word of God.
On the contrary, by setting forth the truth plainly
we commend ourselves to everyone's conscience
in the sight of God.

II Corinthians 4:2

We don't accomplish anything in this world alone . . . and whatever happens is the result of the whole tapestry of one's life and all the weavings of individual threads from one to another that creates something.

Sandra Day O'Connor

NEW THREADS TO FOLLOW

The Lady and the Unicorn, Tracey Chevalier - a charming novel about the creation of tapestries in Flanders during the 15th century.

The Long Journey Home: Understanding and Ministering to the Sexually Abused. Andrew Schmutzer, ed. - contributions focusing on a conversation between psychology, theology and pastoral care on the subject of sexual abuse recovery.

The Secret Life of Bees, the novel by Sue Monk Kidd or the movie by the same name.

tapestry

single strands, diverse and distinctive,
intricately stitched in patterns complex

a myriad of gifts, graciously offered,
eyes that sparkle with a joy unspeakable
that weep with passion and pain;
ears that attend to the harmony of heart,
listening for the troubadour of the soul;
hands that touch with healing and hope;
lips that speak a searing truth,
a gentle rebuke, a comforting peace;
scents of grace, of godliness, of glory;
bread shared, straight from the oven

sisters, friends, women of Christ,
woven together, strong, beautiful,
framed in truth
a King's tapestry.

ABOUT THE AUTHOR

JoAnn Streeter Shade has walked alongside many women in a variety of ministry settings for more than 35 years. She has served in Salvation Army congregations and social service programs, has ministered at North Coast Family Foundation, a Christian counseling center in Northeast Ohio, and has also written extensively about the issues facing women in today's culture.

She is married to Larry, and is the mother of three sons. With an M.A. in pastoral counseling and a D.Min. in the Women in Prophetic Leadership track from Ashland Theological Seminary, she combines her academic training with a writer's eye, a pastor's heart and a grandmother's joy as she serves the body of Christ through Gracednotes Ministries.

She can be reached at gracednotesministries@gmail.com.

www.ingramcontent.com/pod-product-compliance
Lightning Source LLC
Chambersburg PA
CBHW070358290526
45790CB00004B/1538